"Life, the Truth, & Being Free"

Steve Maraboli

"Life, the Truth, & Being Free"

A Better Today Publishing

P.O. Box 1433
Port Washington, NY 11050
(800) 597-9103

www.abettertodaypublishing.com

Originally self-published in 1999 with the name, "Wit and Wisdom of Steve Maraboli"

Renamed and repackaged in 2009 with the name, "Life, the Truth, and Being Free"

15 Year Anniversary Edition published in paperback and e-book in 2014 with updated foreword.

A Better Today Publishing
P.O. Box 1433
Port Washington, NY 11050
(800) 597-9103
www.abettertodaypublishing.com

Cover design by: Chamillah Designs
www.chamillah.com

ISBN 13:   978-1496086242
ISBN 10:   1496086244

Dedicated to the A Better Today Community.

Choose to do more than just exist; choose to live.

Today is a new day!

Table of Contents

Life...

The Truth...

Being Free...

15 Years...

Hi everyone!

Thanks for taking the time to read this book. It's amazing to think that I was just 24 years old when this book was originally published.

Aside from a couple of additions and adjustments in the 10 year anniversary addition, this book was penned during my time serving in the United States Air Force. After serving for four years, I decided to move on from serving as a Military Policeman and begin heading towards my dream of empowering the world with my philosophies and actions.

What a journey it's been! I am honored that this book has done so well and that today finds me one of the most quoted people alive. This is the book that started it all. It was originally a self-published book that I used to hand out at my seminars. When writing these ideas, I don't think I ever considered the material as more than my personal journal. Once I began giving talks, I realized that these ideas were at the base of everything I was saying; that they were my heart and soul to paper.

Today, I'm glad my books are available. I still find that most of the books in the Self-Help section of bookstores belong in the Fiction section. Much of the information is author aggrandizing, pseudo-scientific, and simply not practical. This book, *Life, the Truth, and Being Free,* brings us back to practical empowerment, spirituality, and inspired living.

Many of the pieces in this book have been published and emailed around the world in more than 25 languages. If you listen to my radio shows or have seen me speak live, you will find many of these base philosophies that have become so popular. Among these pages you will find the spiritual, the empowering, the inspirational, and the socially reflective.

My writing style hasn't changed much in the sense that it mirrors my speaking style. My main goal is to convey the message in the most effective manner and I don't overly concern myself with traditional grammatical rules.

Even though this book is split into three parts - Life, the Truth, and Being Free - it is designed to be opened at any page. Also, you will find my popular quotes sprinkled throughout the pages.

Thank you again for joining me in this journey. I appreciate your support more than my words could ever say.

Love and hugs from New York!

-     Steve

Life...

Dare To Be

When a new day begins, dare to smile gratefully.

When there is darkness, dare to be the first to shine a light.

When there is injustice, dare to be the first to condemn it.

When something seems difficult, dare to do it anyway.

When life seems to beat you down, dare to fight back.

When there seems to be no hope, dare to find some.

When you're feeling tired, dare to keep going.

When times are tough, dare to be tougher.

When love hurts you, dare to love again.

When someone is hurting, dare to help them heal.

When another is lost, dare to help them find the way.

When a friend falls, dare to be the first to extend a hand.

When you cross paths with another, dare to make them smile.

When you feel great, dare to help someone else feel great too.

When the day has ended, dare to feel as you've done your best.

Dare to be the best you can –

At all times, Dare to Be!

ഇ൪

Never confuse someone else's inability to do something with its inability to be done.

ഇ൪

The purpose of fear is to raise your awareness, not to stop your progress.

ഇ൪

God's calling requires action. When God calls you, he calls collect... you better be willing to accept the charges of your calling.

ഇ൪

While intent is the seed of manifestation, action is the water that nourishes the seed. Your actions must reflect your goals in order to achieve true success.

ഇ൪

It has been my experience that a bi-product of order is preparedness. And if chance favors the prepared mind, then I am ready!

ഇ൪

We can all fight the battles of just one day. It is when we add the burdens of two uncontrollable days, yesterday and tomorrow, that we get overwhelmed.

ഇ൪

This Moment

Today is a new day!

Each of us aspires to become more. Each of us wants to improve ourselves in some way. Our chance has come! It is time to seize this opportunity to transform ourselves. The time has come to harness the blessed power within us and to use it to transcend from our current existence into a more empowered reality.

What will you do with this moment? It is this, and only this, moment that is yours. What shall be of the fruit of this moment? Will you seize it and empower yourself with its juices? Or will you let this fruitful moment spoil and gamble that you will receive another?

The power found in this moment is immeasurable. It can propel you to success and happiness or chain you to failure and misery. Which would you prefer? Haven't you had this choice before? Which did you choose? We all know that our lives can change in a flash - in a moment. We have become accustomed to being a victim of a moment.

Today is your opportunity to break free of the limiting belief that the moment answers to no one. This moment is yours and yours alone! Take charge, seize this moment and allow it to propel you to the high levels of an empowered life. Allow upon this fertile moment to be planted the seeds of your happiness and success.

Today is a new day.

Seize this moment!

● ● ●

If you want something you've never had, you have to be willing to do something you've never done.

● ● ●

೫ೲ

The value of a moment is immeasurable. The power of just ONE moment can propel you to success and happiness or chain you to failure and misery.

೫ೲ

At any given moment the choice to be happy is present – we just have to choose to be happy.

೫ೲ

If you intend to change, decide what you want and live your life accordingly.

೫ೲ

Life is the definition you give to events that occur.

೫ೲ

Look around you. Everything changes. Everything on this earth is in a continuous state of evolving, refining, improving, adapting, enhancing... changing. You were not put on this earth to remain stagnant.

೫ೲ

Judging is preventing us from understanding a new truth. Free yourself from the rules of old judgments and create the space for new understanding.

೫ೲ

Embrace the Happy Moments

Of Your Life

An innocent giggle from your child.
A good morning kiss from your spouse.
A good report card.
A visit from the tooth fairy.
A great cup of coffee.
A warm, dry pair of boots.
A snow day.
A loving hug.
A timely smile.
A call from a friend.
A car that starts in the morning.
A job to go to.
Family movie night.
Funny moments.
A vacation.
A day off.
A good book.
A cozy chair.
Your favorite slippers.

Happiness can be found in the simple moments along our great journey through life. At any given moment, the choice to be happy is present - we just have to choose to be happy. How often do we allow ourselves the time to really take in the joys of our lives? Do we fully experience the love transferred from a child's embrace or are we more worried about getting to work on time?

Allow yourself to enjoy each happy moment in your life. Take it in - you deserve it! This universe is balanced. God made it that way. There is always plenty to be worried and sad about, but there is equally plenty to be happy and at peace with. The choice is yours. Through my experiences as a personal coach, I've learned that happiness is not the absence of problems - it's the ability to deal with them. It's the ability to enjoy a rose with no mind of the thorn. It's the ability to celebrate a life even though it has passed. It's seeing the flowers even during a rainstorm.

Happiness is the gauge that measures your relationship with God.

Spread your happiness to others and let them spread theirs to you.

Allow yourself to find the great blessings that surround you every day.

Take a moment... Take it all in... Smile...

Today is a new day... A happy day!

You are what you are because it's what you have chosen to be. If you're unhappy, YOU MUST CHANGE FROM THE INSIDE OUT.

Philosophy In Action

How would your life be different if...

You stopped making negative judgmental assumptions about people you encounter?

Let today be the day...

You look for the good in everyone you meet and respect their journey.

So Much to Do

If you have to ask if you've done enough, you haven't. Each day brings with it the opportunity to do more than you did yesterday.

Each day carries in the blessings of abundance and you have unlimited access to all it offers. Imagine a treasure chest, full of the great valuables of life. You have the opportunity to sort through each item and examine it for your use and liking. As you gaze at all the wonderful treasures in the chest you realize how lucky and blessed you are to be in hold of these treasures.

Imagine all those great fortunes and great blessings. Now imagine that at the beginning of the next day, you get another treasure chest to once again do with it as you wish. At the beginning of your day grab hold of your treasure chest – seize it and rejoice of its fortunes.

Hold it sacred and give generously of its bounty.

There is plenty for all.

୫୦୯୫

Today stretches ahead of you waiting to be shaped. You are the sculptor who gets to do the shaping. What today will be like is up to you.

୫୦୯୫

Your actions should be so dedicated that no one should have to ask you what you want.

୫୦୯୫

NEVER be surprised by your own success!

୫୦୯୫

Your agreement with reality defines your life.

୫୦୯୫

Simplify your life. You don't grow spiritual, you shrink spiritual.

୫୦୯୫

Free yourself from the inauthenticity and disempowerment of your story.

୫୦୯୫

Happiness is the gauge that measures your relationship with God.

୫୦୯୫

ℰᴓℭꜱ

Live your vision and demand your success.

ℰᴓℭꜱ

God's word is not just to be heard and repeated; it is to be breathed, lived, and emulated with each action.

ℰᴓℭꜱ

Sometimes the greatest messages come out of the greatest messes.

ℰᴓℭꜱ

Don't sit back and wait for life to happen to you. Have a plan and take the needed steps to create what you want.

ℰᴓℭꜱ

The greatest step towards a life of simplicity is to learn to let go.

ℰᴓℭꜱ

There is nothing more dangerous to the shackles of complacency and the warden of fear than philosophy in action.

ℰᴓℭꜱ

Within ourselves we all have the gifts and talents we need to fulfill the purpose we've been blessed with.

ℰᴓℭꜱ

Create a Masterpiece

Today, you awaken to a day in which you have the power to make and inspire change.

In fact, it is the ONLY day in which you have any power. You have no control over yesterday. Yesterday is gone. Tomorrow is a day you haven't even met, it is beyond our reach. Tomorrow is waiting to reveal itself depending on the actions of just one day... TODAY!

What will you do with today?

Will you continue just existing instead of truly living?

Will you finally break free from the victim mentality and take control of your life?

You have been blessed with immeasurable power to make positive changes in your life. Change things up today!

You will never convince me that we go through everything we go through just to end up where we were when we started. We are here to evolve... to refine and improve ourselves... to inspire and help others to do the same.

Today is a new day!

It's yours to shape. Create a masterpiece!

৪৩

Your dream is a reality that is just waiting for you to materialize it!

৪৩

Although time seems to fly by, it never travels faster than one day at a time. Each day is a new opportunity to live your life to the fullest.

৪৩

When your intent and your actions are aligned, you are speaking directly to God.

৪৩

Attachment is the still water in which the mosquitoes of stress grow.

৪৩

If your vision becomes distorted, your journey becomes delayed.

৪৩

Even if you have been neglecting your body, you'll find that our cells are so much more forgiving than we are. The second you start loving your body, it starts loving you back. It doesn't hold grudges. As soon as you start feeding yourself better emotionally, spiritually, and physically, everything responds in the positive.

৪৩

Do Not Lose Today

This day has been handed to us to shape as we choose. However, this blessing is often overlooked because we tend to focus on the two days in every week that we should not worry about. Two days that dilute our experience of today with an injection of anxiety and fear.

One of these days is yesterday; with all its mistakes and stresses, its victories and losses, its aches and pains. Yesterday has come and passed. There is not a thing you can do to bring back yesterday. We cannot undo anything that happened. We cannot un-say a single word we said. Yesterday is gone.

The other day we should not worry about yet still remains an anxiety and fear-inducing day is tomorrow, with its possible issues, its burdens, its dreams and nightmares. Tomorrow is a day we have yet to touch, it's beyond our control. Tomorrow will greet us with no rules, no resentments, and no promises. Tomorrow will be a day of limitless potential for change, growth, and action, but, until it comes we have no control of tomorrow because we have yet to see it.

This leaves only one day. Our most vital blessing: TODAY!

I'm not saying it's wrong to plan for the future. I'm warning not to make today a victim of those plans.

It's good planning to save for your child's education, but don't forget to enjoy your child today.

Enjoy today, it's what you hold in your senses now. It's what we, as humans, are made to handle. We can all fight the battles of just one day. It is when we add the burdens of two uncontrollable days, yesterday and tomorrow, that we get overwhelmed.

Take a moment for an internal observation of your stresses. So often, it is not the issues of today that crumble your peace of mind. It is more often the ghost of what happened yesterday and the fear and insecurity of what tomorrow may bring.

Do not allow your spirit to be softened, or your happiness to be limited, by a day you cannot have back and a day that does not yet exist.

Forget yesterday – it has already forgotten you. Don't sweat tomorrow – you haven't even met.

Instead, open your eyes and your heart to a truly precious gift, today.

Enjoy it. Live it to the fullest.

Today is a new day!

Philosophy In Action

How would your life be different if...

You stopped focusing on what you didn't want and started focusing on what you do want?

Let today be the day...

You establish a clear intent, make a plan, and take actions towards your intent.

୨୭ଓଃ

Those who are successful give credit to their mistakes and give them a polished new name, experience.

୨୭ଓଃ

There is no greater force for change than people inspired to live a better life.

୨୭ଓଃ

As for biblical or religious theory; I don't ever want to fight about the details of the story, I want to live the reality of the message.

୨୭ଓଃ

God is the architect of the event; you are the interpreter of the moment.

୨୭ଓଃ

You may be keeping a diary of your thoughts, but know that in every religion, the God you believe in is keeping a diary of your actions.

୨୭ଓଃ

Remember that there is an abundance of happiness that can be found in the smallest of places.

୨୭ଓଃ

Live life with a purpose and live it full out.

୨୭ଓଃ

Say "POP!"

We all get to a point in our lives when we need to wake up and snap out of our slump.

I use the term "POP" because it reminds me of a funny story.

Many of you know I'm a military veteran. I was an Air Force Military Policeman for four years, honorably discharged with plenty of medals.

I remember being in basic training in San Antonio, Texas. Basic training consists of endless repetition of drills regardless of the weather. It was a hot Texas summer day and there we all were, sixty of us in one group repeatedly going over our drills on the hot blacktop marching pad.

I remember I felt like I was in a daze. I don't know if it was the intense heat or maybe because we were doing the same thing over and over again, but we were all just kind of going through the motions, and needless to say the drill instructor was furious, yelling at the top if his lungs, but no matter how much he yelled we just couldn't get it right.

So he had us get into formation, he screamed, "Get in formation!"

We all lined up and he paced in front of us, back and forth, and started to speak to us with this thick southern accent.

He said, "What's wrong wit ya'll?"

He continued, "I know... say 'POP!'"

So of course we all repeated, "POP!"

He yelled, "Say POP again!"

And of course we all yelled, "POP" again and before you knew it, there were sixty guys, standing under the hot Texas sun, screaming "POP," "POP," "POP," at the top of their lungs.

The drill instructor then looks at us and says, "Do you know what that is?"

"That's the sound of your heads coming out of your butts!"

I laugh now, but it wasn't so funny back then. But the story stuck with me because it's so true.

In life, sometimes you just have to POP!

You get to a point where you're just going through the motions in life.

Don't you feel that way sometimes?

I know some of you are thinking, "Oh yeah, he's talking to me."

You get to a point where you're just going through the motions and you feel like it's the same thing over and over again.

How many times do you hear somebody say, "Same crap different day," and you're kind of just in a fog, and just existing through every day, or existing through your relationship, or existing through your marriage, or existing through your career? Sometimes you just have to POP, snap out of it, clear your vision, take control, and take command of your life like we did on that hot Texas summer day.

Sometimes the key to LIVING instead of just existing is just a matter of saying, "POP!"

Don't be afraid of your past. Learn from it so it can empower your present.

෨෦ඏ

Time waits for no one. There is only one time for happiness and the time is NOW!

෨෦ඏ

The reason why fear is so powerful is because you believe it to be stronger than you.

෨෦ඏ

Be considerate with the Earth. More people have to use it when you're gone.

෨෦ඏ

You were put on this earth to achieve your greatest self, to live out your purpose, and to do it fearlessly.

෨෦ඏ

No matter what your history has been, your destiny is what you create today. What are you going to create?

෨෦ඏ

Do not let your TODAY be stolen by the ghost of yesterday or the "To-Do" list of tomorrow!

෨෦ඏ

Love in its most genuine sense, can only flourish if it is FREE. We, as people, can only flourish if we are free.

෨෦ඏ

Soul Mate

When we are born, the soul we are given is split apart and half of it is given to someone else. Throughout our lives, we search for the person with the other half of our soul. Very few ever succeed.

I am blessed that we have met. In a sudden moment, warm within your loving glare, my soul said, "At last! I can rest. I have found my missing half." When this happens, it is said we have found our soul mate. We are happy and at peace. When we shared ourselves, we were engulfed in eternity, dancing in a timeless universe. I am truly blessed because that day, my heart recognized you as a part of its own.

Thank you for blessing me with you. Thank you for dreaming with me - for seeing the same future as I do. For your beautiful eyes, reminding me of the truest bliss in life. I am forever grateful for you.

I will spend an eternity loving you, caring for you, respecting you, showing you every day that I hold you as high as the stars.

I am sorry that it's taken me this long to find you – I shall make it up to you, my flower, as long as we live.

I love you!

⮞⮜

Free yourself from the complexities of your life! A life of simplicity and happiness awaits you.

⮞⮜

A lack of clarity could put the brakes on any journey to success.

⮞⮜

Live authentically. Why would you continue to compromise something that's beautiful to create something that is fake?

⮞⮜

I don't want my life to be defined by what is etched on a tombstone. I want it to be defined in what is etched in the lives and hearts of those I've touched.

⮞⮜

In essence, your eyes don't show you what you see, they show you what you believe.

⮞⮜

Nothing is so self-sabotaging as having your actions not reflect your goals. Your life is always just waiting for permission to go where you want it to go... to be shaped how you want it to be shaped.

⮞⮜

Failed Resolutions?

Don't Be Discouraged!

Usually just a few weeks into the New Year I already begin to receive many emails about failed resolutions. So many want to lose weight, earn more money, be a better spouse/companion, be more organized, get better grades, etc.

Although the specifics of each email differ, there is a common question, "Why do I fail if it is something I really want?" Well, it fails because wanting is not enough. Although goals are important, having a plan of action is vital to the success of those goals. Having a goal with no plan of action is like wanting to travel to a new destination without having a map.

Do you want to be successful in your resolutions? Remember, if you keep doing what you're doing, you'll keep getting what you're getting. If you want something new in your life, you have to do something new in your life. Here is a simple outline that is highly effective and a great way to start:

Take the simple steps necessary to empower yourself and enhance your life.

1. Take a moment to quiet your mind.

2. Reflect upon your life and your thoughts.

3. Define your intent. What are your goals? What would you like to change in your life?

4. Write it down! (This is your destination)

5. Have a clear vision of your goals and visualize their realization. (See yourself achieving your goals)

6. Decide upon actions necessary to achieve your goals.

7. Write them down! (This is your map)

8. Take action. Move towards your goal.

9. Maintain clarity of your vision. (It's ok if you have a bad day. A wrong turn does not end the journey. If you feel lost, just look at your map and get back on the road. The map will always lead you in the right direction.)

10. Enjoy your success! Follow the system and you cannot fail!

೮ಿೞ

The only power fear has is the power you give it.

೮ಿೞ

Intent is a reflection of the spirit's desire to create in the material world.

೮ಿೞ

The bank of love is never bankrupt.

೮ಿೞ

God's language is action. For God, faith is a verb.

೮ಿೞ

As for the journey of life: at some point you will realize that YOU are the driver and you will drive!

೮ಿೞ

Listen to what others have to say. When you speak, you're only repeating things you already know. When you listen you learn.

೮ಿೞ

The very thing that is causing you pain is building you up.

೮ಿೞ

Philosophy In Action

How would your life be different if...

You stopped worrying about things you can't control
and started focusing on the things you can?

Let today be the day...

You free yourself from fruitless worry, seize the day
and take effective action on things you can change.

Do Something!

I was sitting on a plane after a long, tiring business trip. I was a bit grouchy and irritable because the rigorous schedule I had made for myself left me exhausted. Looking to not talk to the person next to me and simply endure the flight, I decided to open my newspaper and read about what was happening in the world. As I continued to read, it seemed that everywhere I looked there were stories of injustice, pain, suffering, and people losing hope. Finally, fueled by my tired, irritable state, I became overcome with compassion and frustration for the way things were. I got up and went to the bathroom and broke down.

With tears streaming down my face, I helplessly looked to the sky and yelled to God.

"God, look at this mess. Look at all this pain and suffering. Look at all this killing and hate. God, how could you let this happen? Why don't you do something?"

Just then, a quiet stillness pacified my heart. A feeling of peace I won't ever forget engulfed my body.

And, as I looked into my own eyes in the mirror, the answer to my own question came back to me...

"Steve, stop asking God to do something. God already did something, he gave you life. Now YOU do something!"

෫

If you perceive yourself in a negative manner, then success is next to impossible.

෫

It's thinking you know that stops you from knowing.

෫

Every single time you help somebody stand up you are helping humanity rise.

෫

Come to accept that if your methods don't change, neither will your results.

෫

You have the ability to choose your reactions.

෫

Empowerment is the ability to refine, improve, and enhance your life without co-dependency.

෫

Stop giving meaningless praise and start giving meaningful action.

෫

You and I

When you look at me, your eyes become mine. For I can see what you see and how you see it. You are not alone. Breathe with me; I shall listen to the breath like a melody of love. Together we shall take in new oxygen; a new scoop of life force. Let it spread through your spiritual body. Let it connect with all it may connect with.

Cry with me, for you are not alone. We, together, shall hold firm the ground and bathe in its healing. Sing with me for you and I are one. We can only breathe together. We are the sun, the moon, and the dancing stars.

Fly with me, for we are angels in this spiritual journey. You and I are the same. You and I are one. You are my neighbor, my brother, my sister - let me wrap you in my love and warm you with eternal compassion. You are not alone for you and I are one.

৪৩

Accept yourself, your strengths, your weaknesses, your truths, and connect with the tools you have to fulfill your purpose.

৪৩

Your fear is 100% dependent on you for its survival.

৪৩

A true visionary shows me their vision with their actions.

৪৩

If humans were inclined to goodness, religion would not be necessary.

৪৩

I feel keeping a promise to yourself is a direct reflection of the love you have for yourself. I used to make promises to myself and find them easy to break. Today, I love myself enough to not only make a promise to myself, but I love myself enough to keep that promise.

৪৩

The God we've been praying to is deaf to our words and only responds to our actions.

৪৩

It's Your Season

Every few months one season begins to make its elegant exit as another greets us with its refreshing changes. Change is in the air...

What about you?

Are you going to allow the world around you to change while you remain stagnant?

Why not let this season of change be YOUR season?

Let this be the time when the fresh seasonal transition carries a tune of change that makes your heart dance!

It's YOUR season!

You have been waiting to break free and release your greatest self. Let this be your season.

Enough of the same old rut!

Enough of the worries, insecurities, and doubt!

Enough of the regret!

Enough of letting undeserving people dictate your moods!

Enough of giving others power over you!

Enough of feeling empty and unfulfilled!

Enough of letting days, weeks, months, and years pass without truly embracing all their blessings!

Enough is enough!

Change is in the air. This change reminds us that we are made and beautifully sculpted by the same power that is orchestrating this transition. Let this be the season you embrace and align yourself with this change.

Look around you. Everything changes. Everything on this earth is in a continuous state of evolving, refining, improving, adapting, enhancing... changing. You were not put on this earth to remain stagnant.

It's your season of refinement, enhancement, happiness, and success.

Make this the time you throw away old habits that have hindered your happiness and success and finally allow your greatest self to flourish.

The time has come. YOUR time is now.

It's your season.

And remember, I'm here cheering you on.

The Truth...

Today Is A New Day!

Today is a beautiful day because it's a gift.

Many people around the world did not receive this gift.

You did receive the gift of TODAY – what are you going to do with it?

Today Is A New Day!!

If you want to be a better father or mother – today's the day!

If you want to be a better son or daughter – today's the day!

If you want to forgive those who have wronged you – today's the day!

Yes, this gift is so precious that...

If you want to take steps to improve your health – today's the day!

If you want to help a charity – today's the day!

If you want to pray for a troubled friend – today's the day!

You see, what you do with the gift of TODAY is up to you.

If you want to improve yourself or your life or anyone

else's life in any way, today's the day!!!

Welcome to today!!

Unfortunately, the truth is usually the first casualty in an interaction between two people.

⚘

The power to change your life lies in the simplest of steps.

⚘

There's a difference between having the faith to believe and having the faith to receive.

⚘

You have to create the space for God to fill.

⚘

Plan for your success; Live your success... Act as if.

⚘

There is an abundance of power to be found in simplicity.

⚘

Enjoy today, it's what you hold in your senses now.

⚘

You sing the song in your heart and the people it resonates with are going to dance to it.

⚘

Religious structure often dilutes the spiritual experience.

⚘

G Is For Gratitude

I know sometimes it is difficult to be grateful. I know that sometimes it is difficult to be happy. If you're reading a book that's telling you that you should always be happy, put away the book.

You're a human being, you're a dimensional creature, you're multi-dimensional. You are not one dimensional. It is impossible for you to always be happy. There is no such thing as a one-sided magnet.

Being content, now that's a different story.

I want you all to realize that this universe is balanced. Whether you look at it as a scientific point of view and you say, "Well, to every action, there's an equal and opposite reaction and everything has to have peaks and valleys," or you can look at it in the spiritual way where you say, "God has balanced the universe, there is good and there is bad and there's God and there's the Devil," whichever way you want to look at it. The truth is, the universe is balanced.

You will always be given the choice to celebrate that thorns have roses or to complain that roses have thorns. You will always be given that choice.

I'm asking you to choose gratitude.

What does that mean? It simply means that you choose to empower your agreement with reality. I'm asking you, if you look at your situation, could you possibly be seeing it in a disempowering manner?

Are you seeing your situation properly? How are you seeing it?

Is it your interpretation of your situation that's making you miserable?

Remember, energy attracts energy, so if you're miserable in your situation because you're not grateful then you're attracting more negative energy toward you.

So, what are you grateful for?

One of my favorite writers, Byron Katie, suggests you make a list. Start with 100, then 1,000, then 10,000.

You'll be surprised once you get into it. When you sit and think about it, there are so many things that you can be grateful for in your life.

Also, you get a bit of insight to things you may not have been seeing; valuable seeds that you were not recognizing.

In the Bible, the children of Israel were enslaved and they kept asking for a warrior, a soldier to come get them out of slavery, and God sends Moses. But see, Moses didn't come as a warrior or soldier, Moses came as a baby. Moses came as a baby and nobody recognized that the warrior, the one who would stand up to Pharaoh, was this helpless baby. Nobody knew that this seed was everything they asked for. They didn't recognize the value of that seed.

Let's begin to observe and recognize the value of the seeds in our lives.

A grateful mindset can set you free from the prison of disempowerment and the shackles of misery.

Do you see an acorn or an oak tree?

You have to realize that the tree is in the seed.

The hawk, the eagle, is in the egg.

That's the way it happens.

So many people are into the Law of Attraction these days, so it helps to understand that your seed is that initial intent and it comes to pass when your actions reflect that intent.

You have to recognize the value of the seed.

When you're grateful for something, like the emails I get from the people who were affected by Hurricane Katrina, they say, "At first, I was miserable because I lost my house. What I hadn't realized is that if I hadn't lost my house, I wouldn't have been forced to go back to school, and now I have a better job. If I hadn't lost that house, I would have never been forced to get my children out of this neighborhood and now we live in a better neighborhood. It was bad for a while, but only because I wasn't seeing the situation clearly. I wasn't open to the possibility that something good could come out of this tragedy."

My life is not unlike yours. Believe me, I go through the same things you all go through. You go through heartache and stresses and through issues of dealing with people, I go through all of that just like you do. I too have relatives, some are nice and some are not nice. I have friends and acquaintances, some are nice, some are not nice, some use you, some don't. I experience the same stuff you all do. I'm on the same earth you're on and we all experience the same things.

What I have realized is that any time I thought I was in a horrible situation, it turned out that what I thought was my worst situation was actually my greatest teacher.

I learned that the greatest messages in my life have come out of the greatest messes.

I'm asking you, could you be looking at your situation in a negative and ungrateful manner? What is the message in your situation and are you grateful for that message?

No situation comes labeled. YOU are the labeler. There is a truth I will share with you that has been a pillar in my success. That truth is: Nothing can happen to me... Nothing can happen on this beautiful earth that God hasn't allowed. I find peace in that truth. I find strength in knowing that everything is in alignment with our perfectly evolving universe. My job is to recognize the value of the seeds.

So look at your life and your situation. Be grateful. There is a good message God is whispering in your ear. I know it because this universe is balanced. It cannot be any other way.

Have a goal, a destination, and a clear map. If you don't know where you are going, any road will take you there.

Philosophy In Action

How would your life be different if...

You pretended those around you were
deaf to your words?

Let today be the day...

You let your actions speak and communicate
your feelings and intentions.

৪৩৫

Sometimes the prison of fear is so powerful there's no need to lock the cell doors. Your fear creates a willingness to self-imprison.

৪৩৫

A bruise to the ego often hurts more than a break to the bone.

৪৩৫

We will get true and lasting change as soon as we make helping people a way of life instead of a business.

৪৩৫

It doesn't matter what you did or where you were, it matters where you are and what you're doing.

৪৩৫

If you are not in the now you are nowhere.

৪৩৫

There is nothing more beautiful than seeing a person being themselves. Imagine going through your day being unapologetically you.

৪৩৫

ഉരു

You can't just wish change; you have to live the change in order for it to become a reality.

ഉരു

The true dynamic of a successful friendship and relationship is when the respect is mutual and reciprocal.

ഉരു

When we focus our attention on things that are either in the past or in the future, it dilutes our experience of right now. Today is the day you can break free from that.

ഉരു

Life doesn't get easier or more forgiving; we get stronger and more resilient.

ഉരു

Nothing is as unpopular as the truth.

ഉരു

Today is yours to shape. Create a masterpiece!

ഉരു

The right thing to do and the hard thing to do are usually the same thing.

ഉരു

Why Not You?

Today, many will awaken with a fresh sense of inspiration. Why not you?

Today, many will open their eyes to the beauty that surrounds them. Why not you?

Today, many will choose to leave the ghost of yesterday behind and seize the immeasurable power of today. Why not you?

Today, many will break through the barriers of the past by looking at the blessings of the present. Why not you?

Today, for many, the burden of self doubt and insecurity will be lifted by the security and confidence of empowerment. Why not you?

Today, many will rise above their believed limitations and make contact with their powerful innate strength. Why not you?

Today, many will choose to live in such a manner that they will be a positive role model for their children. Why not you?

Today, many will choose to free themselves from the personal imprisonment of their bad habits. Why not you?

Today, many will choose to live free of conditions and rules governing their own happiness. Why not you?

Today, many will find abundance in simplicity. Why not you?

Today, many will be confronted by difficult moral choices and they will choose to do what is right instead of what is beneficial. Why not you?

Today, many will decide to no longer sit back with a victim mentality, but to take charge of their lives and make positive changes. Why not you?

Today, many will take the action necessary to make a difference. Why not you?

Today, many will make the commitment to be a better mother, father, son, daughter, student, teacher, worker, boss, brother, sister, and so much more. Why not you?

Today is a new day!

Many will seize this day.

Many will live it to the fullest.

Why not you?

ഇൻൽ

Happiness is not the absence of problems; it's the ability to deal with them.

ഇൻൽ

There is a universal law: INTENT is the cause, your life is the effect.

ഇൻൽ

Your greatest self has been waiting your whole life; don't make it wait any longer.

ഇൻൽ

Social thinking dilutes most personal power.

ഇൻൽ

Today is the only day in which we have any power.

ഇൻൽ

Give yourself entirely to those around you. Be generous with your blessings. A kind gesture can reach a wound that only compassion can heal.

ഇൻൽ

Your simple smile can lighten the darkest places.

ഇൻൽ

The Five Truths

Truth #1: Today is the Only Day in Which We Have Any Power.

There are two days in every week that we need not worry about. While they remain the most popular days to stress over and the most anxiety and fear inducing days, they also remain the days in which you have absolutely no power.

One of these days is yesterday, with all its mistakes and worries, its highs and lows, its aches and pains. Yesterday has passed. Nothing in the world can bring back yesterday. We cannot undo a single thing that happened. We cannot erase a single word we said. Yesterday is gone.

The other day we should not worry about is tomorrow, with its possible problems, its burdens, its dreams and nightmares. Tomorrow is a day we have yet to touch, it's beyond our control. Tomorrow, the sun will rise and greet us with no rules, no restrictions and unlimited opportunities. However, we have no control of tomorrow because we have yet to see it.

This leaves only one day. Our most vital blessing: TODAY!

I'm not saying it's wrong to plan for the future. I'm warning not to make today a victim of those plans.

Enjoy today, it's what you hold in your senses now. It's what we, as humans, are made to handle. *It is the ONLY day in which we have any power.* We can all fight the battles of just one day. It is when we add the burdens of two uncontrollable days, yesterday and tomorrow, that we get overwhelmed.

Take a moment for an internal observation of your stresses. So often, it is not the issues of today that crumble your peace of mind. It is more often the ghost of what happened yesterday and the fear and insecurity of what tomorrow may bring.

Do not allow your spirit to be softened or your happiness to be limited by a day you cannot have back and a day that does not yet exist.

Forget yesterday – it has already forgotten you. Don't sweat tomorrow – you haven't even met.

Instead, open your eyes and your heart to a truly precious gift – today.

Seize it! Enjoy it! Live it to the fullest!

Today is a new day!

Truth #2: Your Agreement with Reality Defines Your Life.

I have heard so many people ask the philosophical question, "What is life?" I'll tell you what it is. Life is the definition you give to events that occur. I'll say it again. Life is the definition you give to events that occur.

Life is defined by an individual's labels. That's why you may hear so many answers to that philosophical question.

Some people say, life's tough, life's a party, life's a beach, life's a classroom, life stinks, life's a dance, etc... Life is and can be all these things and more. It depends on the individual and their agreement with reality.

You see, no event in life comes labeled, you alone are the labeler. It's true, some people see a stumbling block, and others see a stepping stone. Which is true? BOTH. It depends on that person's agreement with reality. If they define it as a stumbling block, then that's what it will be and they will struggle with it. If they define it as a stepping stone, then that is what it will be and they'll succeed.

You will always define events in a manner which will validate your agreement with reality.

In other words, if an individual has a victim mentality, their agreement with reality is one that will see a stumbling block, and when it keeps them from succeeding they will say, "You see, I knew I couldn't do it." Or "I knew something would go wrong." They will validate their agreement with reality and it will define their life.

What's your agreement with reality? You must take a conscious look at your agreement with reality. If it perceives you in a negative manner, success is next to impossible.

On the other hand, if you can transcend from the dark rut of disempowered thinking to the bright light of an empowered agreement with reality, you will see opportunities not barriers.

You will see the finish line, not the hurdles.

You will no longer complain that roses have thorns but will celebrate that thorns have roses.

That's empowered thinking.

Truth #3: There is a Difference between Believing and Knowing.

If you believe you can, you might. If you know you can, you will.

The word belief implies question. By definition there is a degree of uncertainty. Think about it, if you believe with certainty, then you wouldn't say, "I believe", you would say, "I KNOW."

To know is to be certain. There is no question in knowing. There can be no doubt found when you KNOW something.

When you come to understand this truth and apply it to your agreement with reality, the improvement in your ability and likelihood to succeed is immeasurable.

I am a person who walks in the knowing of their ability, takes calculated, purpose-driven steps towards a goal they know they will reach.

I'm reminded of a story I once heard about a community.

The story goes like this...

Several years ago, a small farming community was experiencing a terrible drought. The leaders of the community called a prayer meeting in hope of everyone attending and holding a group prayer for rain.

One man was in attendance with his small son. As everyone was praying, the small boy reached up and tugged his father's shirt to ask, "Daddy, what is everyone doing?" The man explained that everyone was praying for rain and they believed it would help. The father went back to his prayer.

The boy looked around for a few more minutes and was puzzled. He tugged again on his dad's shirt and asked, "Daddy, if everyone is here to pray for rain, and they believe it will happen, why didn't anyone bring an umbrella?"

Now take a moment to think about it...

What do you think will be more effective when it comes to succeeding, believing you can or KNOWING you will?

Let today be the last day you took timid steps of belief and start taking confident steps of purpose-driven knowing!

Truth #4: Change is the Parent of Progress.

If you keep doing what you're doing, you'll keep getting what you're getting. Without change, progress is impossible.

If you think about it, it is ridiculous to do the same thing over and over again and expect something to change. But how many of us have done this? How many of us continue to do this?

It's time for a change! Today you have an opportunity to align your actions with your goals.

It is important that when we make a resolution, or establish a goal, that we take the ACTION necessary to accomplish that goal. You cannot continue on the same path and arrive at a different destination. Make the choice to have your actions reflect your goals.

Shake it up. Do something different. Take planned, calculated steps towards a new goal, or a new you. It's the only way to ensure that you won't get the same results in your life.

It's been said that when Thomas Edison was experimenting with the light bulb, he had done 1,000 tests that produced no results. When challenged about it, Edison said, "Actually, I have had plenty of results. I now know 1,000 things that DON'T work."

You too already know what DOESN'T work, so stop doing it!

The formula is simple, do something different and you'll get something different.

Choose to shape and follow your new path!

Truth #5: Your Actions Must Reflect Your Goals.

When it comes to success, change, achievement, and living your purpose, intent is vital. Because of this, intent is often given 100% of the credit for success, change, and the "manifestation" of the ideal life. In this thought process, an unfortunate casualty is an equally vital but less popular component of life enhancement, action.

If intent was enough, if it was all you needed to get what you want, if wanting something with your heart and visualizing it was enough, if putting up pictures of your goal or desire was enough, if meditating on it was enough, then every teenager would be driving a speedy sports car, playing on a pro sports team, or singing in a band.

But the truth is intent alone is simply not enough. Think about it, how many people do you know who WANT to be in a different situation than they are in but seem to still take the same actions that got them there in the first place? Of course their intent for positive change is there, but there is no action reflecting that goal and because of that, there is no progress and no change.

Only when your intent and actions are in alignment can you create the reality you desire. While intent is the seed of manifestation, action is the water that nourishes the seed. Your actions must reflect your goals in order to achieve true success.

If you want to succeed, make a plan and take actions that reflect your goals.

Action is the universal language of success.

Sometimes the greatest messages are found in the greatest messes.

☙❧

Love has no limitations. It cannot be measured. It has no boundaries. Although many have tried, love is indefinable.

☙❧

Nothing is going to change unless you first change.

☙❧

When you find yourself in need of spiritual nourishment, it is in the opportunities to serve others that you will find the abundance you seek.

☙❧

Today greets you in the morning with an embrace and a kiss. How will you greet it back?

☙❧

Freedom is more than just a word and a patriotic concept; it is the purest intent of God.

☙❧

I don't think we are ever prepared for the level of warfare at which ignorance fights.

☙❧

My mistakes have been my greatest mentors.

☙❧

୫୬

It is only with true love and compassion that we can begin to mend what is broken in the world. It is only these two blessed things that can begin to heal all the broken hearts.

୫୬

Those who have the ability to be grateful are the ones who have the ability to achieve greatness.

୫୬

How would your life change if your actions did all the talking and all you used your mouth for was to say please and thank you?

୫୬

Remember, nothing in life comes labeled, YOU are the labeler.

୫୬

At the end of the day, let there be no excuses, no explanations, no regrets.

୫୬

I am not arrogant enough to tell you what the future holds, but I am faithful enough to remind you who holds the future.

୫୬

Pretend God is Deaf

Learning the Language of God

Being raised Catholic and having read the scriptures many times, I had always privately wondered about and even questioned the nature of God and the power of prayer.

I would wonder why, even though millions around the world have prayed for peace, there has always been war. Why countless people have prayed for health, but have just been surrounded by disease. Why so many have prayed for abundance, but have experienced famine. I couldn't help but privately question why an ever-loving God would ignore such requests.

One day, in a moment of frustration, I had a revelation. I quickly looked back at scriptures and even thought about my own life and prayers I felt weren't answered. I realized that maybe it wasn't that they we never answered but instead, were never heard.

You see, I came to a realization that the language of God is action. Even though it has been a popular idea to make God similar to the old myths of a genie in a bottle who simply grants wishes to a passerby, that representation of God isn't supported by anything neither written nor experienced.

God is deaf to your words. God is deaf to anything that isn't action driven. We have been produced by this majestic creator with all the tools we need to deliver commanding prayers with our actions. This isn't a God who simply wants you on your knees praying in vain; he wants you up on your feet and living the prayer.

Now I finally understand why Jesus told his disciples that, "When you pray and ask for something, act as if you have already received it and you will be given whatever you ask."

How would your life be different if you were to pretend God is deaf? How would things change if you change the language in which you spoke to God? What if instead of just praying for peace, you lived peace... instead of praying for health, you lived health... instead of praying for success, you lived success?

What if you acted as if or became the very thing you were praying for?

Love, Peace, Success, Health... these are not things you have, they are not just to be hoped for, they are not miracles to be begged for; these are things you experience when you live accordingly. They are not something you have, they are something you do.

Philosophy In Action

How would your life be different if...

You renamed your "To-Do" list to your
"Opportunities" list?

Let today be the day...

You look at each day as a treasure chest filled with
limitless opportunities and take joy in
checking many off your list.

ℰℛ

A wrong turn doesn't end the journey. If you feel lost, just look at your map and get back on the road. The map will always lead you in the right direction.

ℰℛ

The empowered mind gravitates towards freedom and helps you break free of all limitations.

ℰℛ

A life by choice is one that is filled with love, happiness, and an appreciation of each day.

ℰℛ

When you do what you love, the seemingly impossible becomes simply challenging, the laborious becomes purposeful resistance, the difficult loses its edge and is trampled by your progress.

ℰℛ

I've learned that empowered thinking is a choice – a state of mind. It's the ability to enjoy a rose with no mind of the thorn. It's the ability to celebrate a life even though it has passed. It's seeing the flowers even during a rainstorm.

ℰℛ

Let the glow in your heart reflect in your soul.

ℰℛ

One Day at a Time

It seems everybody is really busy these days. I understand that at times the stresses of work and family make it easy to lose focus and make each day a blur. My life is not unlike yours. I too seem to have a mountain of work to move but only a spoon with which to dig. But I want to share with you a simple TRUTH that helps me accomplish what I need to do while at the same time never losing focus.

Although time seems to fly, it never travels faster than one day at a time. Each day is a new opportunity to live your life to the fullest. In each waking day, you will find scores of blessings and opportunities for positive change. Do not let your TODAY be stolen by the ghost of yesterday or the "To-Do" list of tomorrow!

Harness the power of today. Seize the blessings of today! Make something happen, enhance your life, make someone laugh, help a friend, love, love, love!

Choose to do it - TODAY!

Today is a new day!

⅋⅋

It only takes a split second to smile and forget, yet to someone that needed it, it can last a lifetime. We should all smile more often.

⅋⅋

Search for contentment in each person you meet.

⅋⅋

I'm not saying it's wrong to plan for the future. I'm warning not to make today a victim of those plans.

⅋⅋

Happiness has to do with your mindset, not with outside circumstance.

⅋⅋

In a strong relationship, you should love your companion more than you need them.

⅋⅋

It is important that we forgive ourselves for making mistakes. We need to learn from our errors and move on.

⅋⅋

Identify the things and people that make you feel unhappy and eliminate them from your life. Nothing good can come from them.

⅋⅋

Your Truth and Your Circumstance

Who are you?

All too often, we put our attention on things that blind us from the truth of our true self. We lose sight of our position in life and forget that we are children of God, individually created with the tools we need to fulfill our purpose.

Instead of staying focused on the truth of our divine position, we tend to look at and give power to our temporary circumstance. We then identify with this circumstance and confuse it for our truth.

"I'm fat, I'm broke, I'm divorced, I'm an alcoholic, etc..."

These are not our true position! They are temporary circumstances that, if we focus on and give power to, will blind us to our true greatness and purpose. When you identify with these circumstances and not your truth, it is easy to feel powerless, overwhelmed, and depressed.

Are you feeling stuck in a rut? Are you sick of being in that "same crap - different day" mindset?

When a temporary circumstance blinds you to the beauty and power of your true position, it's easy to fall into a frustrating and disempowering mindset.

It is when you understand your true position that you can effectively manage any circumstance. When you realize that although the circumstance exists, you are not your circumstance, you can break free from that disempowered mindset and live in alignment with your truth.

You are here for a purpose; a position that God has placed you in. Live it today!

Stop being a victim of your own circumstance.

෨෬

It is when we hurt that we learn.

෨෬

The innate power you possess to achieve your dreams is immeasurable.

෨෬

You cannot just speak change, you have to LIVE change!

෨෬

Stress is like a pulse, if you have it you're alive.

෨෬

Sometimes you have to take those first steps, take that leap of faith, and inspire God to catch you.

෨෬

Free yourself from the imprisonment of your own limiting beliefs and prejudices.

෨෬

When you're ready to make the change and you don't feel that you have the strength, know that you are connected with the same strength that moves the world; you just have to stop turning your back on it and connect with it.

෨෬

Fear is the imaginary response to something that has not happened.

Beyond Intention

Intent is a reflection of the spirit's desire to create in the material world. The only way to clearly translate that desire into physical reality is through action. Intent without dedicated action is simply not enough. Action without a clear intent is a waste. It is when these two powerful forces are aligned that the energy of the universe conspires in your favor.

Intent and action are the fuel and vehicle in the journey of creation. When you establish a destination by defining what you want, then take physical action by making choices that move you towards that destination, the possibility for success is limitless and arrival at the destination is inevitable.

Balance these two powerful forces in your life! Too much intent coupled with too little action is a recipe for frustration and impotent existing. Too much action with too little intent makes for wasteful exertion of energy and the confusion between movement and progress. It is in the balance of these forces that the seeds of happiness, success, and creation are watered and nourished to grow.

Today is your day to harness these mega powers and put their limitless potential to work for you. The universe conspires in your favor the moment you deliver to it a clear message of balanced intent and action. Deliver your message today!

Philosophy In Action

How would your life be different if...

You stopped validating your victim mentality?

Let today be the day...

You shake off your self-defeating drama and embrace your innate ability to recover and achieve.

The Ego:

A Celebration of You

So many writers and philosophers discuss the ego and often debate whether you should embrace it or "free" yourself from it. But how do we define the ego? Does it have to be self aggrandizement or selfishness or can it simply be a celebration and identification of self?

I love landscape art and photography. I am often left breathless by the beauty of this wonderful earth, from the amazing sunrise that explodes in a multicolor celebration of a new day to the serene sunset with its blissful whisper of the day's transition; from the majestic mountain ranges to the white sand beaches; from the powerful oceans to the beautiful fields of flowers. I love to see and celebrate all the beauty in this enchantingly hand-sculpted earth that God has blessed us with.

I know I'm not alone in this admiration of beauty. All over the world people have pictures and paintings in their homes of some of these earthly scenes. In museums, the work of artists who capture this beauty is prominently displayed and many people pay to see and admire their work.

So let me ask you this: if it is alright to recognize and celebrate the work of artists, if it's alright to celebrate something a human made, why would you not celebrate something God made? God made you. God hand sculpted you to fulfill a purpose here on this great earth. You are just as majestic as the mountains and just as beautiful as a field of flowers. I believe having an ego is simply recognizing and celebrating the work of God.

This doesn't mean you should be selfish. It doesn't mean you should consider yourself better than anyone else. It means you are an individual and it's ok to recognize that God made you as an individual with a purpose. Don't turn your back on that truth, embrace it and celebrate it!

Thank you for being you!

Today, many will awaken with a fresh sense of inspiration. Why not you?

ഩരു

Being attached to the problems of yesterday or the insecurities of tomorrow will destroy your today.

ഩരു

Your perceptions create your reality.

ഩരു

Embrace your spirituality, but don't turn your back on your humanity.

ഩരു

Forget yesterday – it has already forgotten you. Don't sweat tomorrow – you haven't even met. Instead, open your eyes and your heart to a truly precious gift – today.

ഩരു

In this busy world, we should never be a stranger to love and compassion. It is the fertile soil in the garden of peace.

ഩരു

We must transcend the illusion that money or power has any bearing on our worthiness as children of God.

ഩരു

Change is the parent of progress.

ഩരു

৪৩

Reading the Bible will help you get to know the word, but it's when you put it down and live your life that you get to know the author.

৪৩

When you're in love, your soul feels healthy.

৪৩

Regret is a spiritual scar.

৪৩

Don't be afraid of your past. Learn from it so it can empower your present.

৪৩

Fear can only grow in darkness. Once you face fear with light, you win.

৪৩

Hiding from your history only shackles you to it. Instead, face it and free yourself.

৪৩

It's inspiring to see all the wonderfully amazing things that can happen in a day in which you participate.

৪৩

Relationships

Why are you so full of Shit?!

Reflections from an airport... I'm here an hour and a half early for my flight back to NY, so I'm sitting here at my gate watching all the people walk by. It's amazing the things you can pick up by people watching. You can almost feel the stress on some while you can't help but smile at the happiness of others.

I had no intention of breaking out my laptop and writing. I had an action-packed trip that allotted very little down time so I was content just people watching and reflecting on the events of this trip. But as I was sitting here, a couple walked by and they were clearly in an argument. As tension seemed to escalate, I (and anyone else within a 50 foot radius) heard the woman exclaim, "Why are you so full of shit?"

Her very valid question got me thinking about relationships and honesty. And of course, out came the laptop and here I go.

So here's my brief rant on relationships and honesty.

I'm blessed in what I do in that I get to meet people all across the world and build relationships with them. Whether they are business relationships or personal relationships, I'm always in a process of relationship building. Throughout the years, time and time again I have encountered an excessive amount of people who are just fake.

I know it's not just me. Haven't you also encountered this "Fake People" phenomenon? Some are overtly fake and you can see through their act from a thousand miles away. Others have refined their talent for fictional living to the point where it's almost undetectable.

I'm not sure why people are so quick to lie to others. I'm sure they have some sort of victimized way of justifying it to themselves, but I want to offer a bit of advice.

Here's an idea... When entering into any type of relationship, whether it's one that is going to last one hour or one year or longer, just be honest.

Sounds simple, but for some reason, honesty tends to be the first victim of an interaction between two people.

It's not nice to be dishonest with others, but let's leave the effect on others alone for a second. Let's focus on ourselves.

Why be dishonest? Why compromise yourself so easily?

Why enter into any relationship knowing that you're building it on sand?

If you're not comfortable enough with yourself or with your own truth when entering a relationship, then you're not ready for that relationship. Don't make the other person suffer for your own lack of integrity or inability to embrace the truths of your life. Just because you are available for a relationship doesn't mean you are ready for one.

Be open to developing authenticity in all of your relationships. Building any relationship on a solid foundation of truth greatly increases its chances of longevity... and it may save you a hollering at an airport. ☺

It is those who can see the invisible that can do the impossible.

ৰেড়

The nourishment of our souls comes from the smiles of others.

ৰেড়

The ability to passionately express opposing opinions is the greatest sign of a healthy democracy.

ৰেড়

I'm no longer being paralyzed by your opinion, I'm moving forward with my truth.

ৰেড়

Finding happiness should not be seen as finding a needle in a haystack. Happiness is within. Each day is a blessing that brings an abundance of happiness. Therefore, finding happiness should be like finding a gift in a stack of gifts.

ৰেড়

My life is far too precious and my mission too important to allow either to be chaotically diluted by a lack of order.

ৰেড়

Do not allow yourself to be damaged by your self.

ৰেড়

Perfectly Imperfect

We have all heard that no two snowflakes are alike. Each snowflake takes the perfect form for the maximum efficiency and effectiveness for its journey. And while the universal force of gravity gives them a shared destination, the expansive space in the air gives each snowflake the opportunity to take their own path. They are on the same journey, but each takes a different path.

Along this gravity-driven journey, some snowflakes collide and damage each other, some collide and join together, some are influenced by wind... there are so many transitions and changes that take place along the journey of the snowflake. But, no matter what the transition, the snowflake always finds itself perfectly shaped for its journey.

I find parallels in nature to be a beautiful reflection of grand orchestration. One of these parallels is of snowflakes and us. We, too, are all headed in the same direction. We are being driven by a universal force to the same destination. We are all individuals taking different journeys and along our journey, we sometimes bump into each other, we cross paths, we become altered... we take different physical forms. But at all times we too are 100% perfectly imperfect. At every given moment we are absolutely perfect for what is required for our journey. I'm not perfect for your journey and you're not perfect for my journey, but I'm perfect for my journey and you're perfect for your journey. We're heading to the same place, we're taking different routes, but we're both exactly perfect the way we are.

Think of what understanding this great orchestration could mean for relationships. Imagine interacting with others knowing that they too each share this parallel with the snowflake. Like you, they are headed to the same place and no matter what they may appear like to you, they have taken the perfect form for their journey. How strong our relationships would be if we could see and respect that we are all perfectly imperfect for our journey.

ഇറ

*The most powerful relationship
you will ever have is the
relationship with yourself.*

ഇറ

ഇരു

If you want something you've never had, you have to be willing to do something you've never done.

ഇരു

Have a goal, a destination, and a clear map. If you don't know where you're going, any road will take you there.

ഇരു

Just because you are available for a relationship doesn't mean you are ready for one.

ഇരു

Intent paired with action builds the bridge to success. You can't just want it; you have to do it, live it... BE it!

ഇരു

When you say "I" and "my" too much, you lose the capacity to understand the "we" and "our".

ഇരു

One of the most spiritual things you can do is embrace your humanity.

ഇരു

When we are judging everything, we are learning nothing.

ഇരു

৪০০৪

One of the most spiritual things you can do is acknowledge the human aspect of your life. Once you acknowledge the human aspect of your life you'll recognize the spiritual fuel that ignites that human engine.

৪০০৪

I want to be in a relationship where you telling me you love me is just a ceremonious validation of what you already show me.

৪০০৪

There is an unlimited amount of power to be found in simplicity. Keep your intent and action simple and the doors of success, happiness, and abundance will fly open for you.

৪০০৪

The art of letting go is simply about personal empowerment. Realizing what you're in charge of, realizing what you control, and more importantly, what you don't control.

৪০০৪

Gratitude enhances your ability to see beauty. It's like seeing beauty in HD.

৪০০৪

The Empowered Hypothesis

Today I will wake up with the hypothesis that I am very blessed and capable of breathing change into my life, and over the course of the day, I will have fun continuously proving this hypothesis true.

I will look for the blessings of the day. I will no longer remain blind to the opportunities that surround me. I will take action on change I envision for myself.

On this day of empowered hypothesis, I will turn my "To-Do" list into an "Opportunities Available" list and as I check off each, I will transfer them to another list called "Blessings of this Day".

I will be generous with my love today. I will sprinkle compliments and uplifting words everywhere I go. I will do this knowing that my words are like seeds and when they fall on fertile soil, a reflection of those seeds will grow into something greater.

I will mute the venomous self-talk in my mind. I will cancel its membership to the club of my spirit. I will evict it from the place it has held in my life. No more waking up with the poisonous theory of "same crap different day." Influential negative self-talk has no home in my hypothesis.

Yes, on this beautiful new day I will begin with the hypothesis of greatness and limitless potential. This will be an amazing day, filled with blessings and opportunities to change. I will exhaust myself in the fun of validating this grand hypothesis! Then, I will do it again tomorrow.

Attachment is the still water in which the mosquitoes of stress grow.

☙❧

Be happy with who you are and what you do, and you can do anything you want.

☙❧

This magical universe is so faithful in waiting for us to get out of our own way. Many people do not realize that the sharpening of wit occurs when one humbles their wit. It is in the humble mindset that beauty and magic flow freely.

☙❧

All resistance bears within it the seeds of growth, experience, and wisdom.

☙❧

It's a lack of clarity that creates chaos and frustration. Those emotions are poison to any living goal.

☙❧

Just an observation: it is impossible to be both grateful and depressed. Those with a grateful mindset tend to see the message in the mess. And even though life may knock them down, the grateful find reasons, if even small ones, to get up.

☙❧

The greatest enemy to fear is truth.

☙❧

The Four Pillars of Success

Intent: Determine what you specifically want.

Vision: See it clearly and brightly.

Action: Write down a plan and actively follow it.

Clarity: Maintaining focus and connection to your plan.

The Four Pillars of Success is a system I have been using for over a decade to create my own success and the success of my clients. Having refined and enhanced it throughout the years, I know it is the most practical and solid way to establish, visualize, and reach your goals. The four pillars are the base of success.

Intent

Define your intent. What do you want? People are so used to talking about what they don't want, but that isn't helpful when it comes to forward progress. What you need to establish is a clear, defined goal or destination.

When you establish your intent, do it slowly. It is important that your intent is specific.

Much like the choosing a specific destination on a map, being specific with your intent will facilitate your ability to map out the roads you will take and the means in which you will arrive. Not knowing the specific destination will lead to time loss and frustration. If you don't know exactly where you're going, how will you know when you get there?

Vision

Vision is crucial because it is how you ground your intent. It's how you bring a dream into the realm of the real. If you have a goal, you need to be able to see yourself as having achieved that goal. It has to be something you are able to see yourself doing it. Some of the greatest athletes of all time will tell you, "By the time you saw me run the race I had already run it in my mind a thousand times." They have already visualized what they intend to do, and that is what makes it real.

Think about the kind of house you want to live in and see yourself there. Some people can visualize themselves mowing the lawn or painting the walls, or opening the back door to see their spouse and kids playing together on the swings in the backyard. They visualize every detail because there's no way you'll convince them this isn't happening.

When you visualize your goal, visualize yourself as if it were true. Take some time to create your vision. I know in this day and age, it's hard to get in touch with your thoughts, with the TV and the Internet and all the activity of your life getting between you and your thoughts. But you have to take the time to sit with your thoughts and create your vision. See it as real; be it as if it were real.

Action

This pillar has two parts; writing it down, and taking physical action. At this point, you know your intent. You've created your vision. Time to create the blueprint or map and get to work!

What you write down must be detailed, just like a blueprint for a house - or even a map for getting to somewhere specific. Think of it. Could you imagine engineers attempting to build a structure without a blueprint? Or how about if you get invited to a home where you haven't been before, would you just get in the car and will yourself to end up there? Of course not, that's totally ridiculous. You find out where they live and you *write it down*. Then you base how you're going to get there by seeing where you are, and drawing a course of direction from there. Achieving your goals is exactly the same.

Are you really going to get into the vehicle of your life and start driving around without a map? It's time to use these pillars and start living with direction and focus.

Clarity

Once you've made your plan, the biggest challenge is going to be to get up off your butt and go through with it. Clarity is the key to staying on point and dedicated to your journey. Clarity is vital to the nourishment of your living goals. The lack of clarity is food for failure. Many people give up on their goals simply because the clarity of the vision is lost. That is why it is vital to have a specific intent and a clear vision. A plan that is written from a clear vision is easy to refer back to and to maintain clarity with. Just like referring back to a roadmap when you are traveling, your own success map will provide the information you need and the clarity to finish successfully.

Using the Four Pillars of Success:

There was an abandoned lot of land for years in my home town. Every day I would drive by this patch of land that no one seemed to use or care anything about. But one day, a sign went up, and on this sign was a huge vibrant picture of a beautiful shopping center depicted in amazing detail. In this picture, not only could you see the shopping center, the display windows, and the names of the stores, but you could see the lights, the parking lot lined with spaces, and even birds were depicted flying gracefully above this amazing idea. In what was a seemingly uncared for piece of land now sat this amazing picture, and underneath the picture, a sign with two words: "Coming Soon."

I continued to drive by this lot and noticed the advances of each day. A giant hole was dug for a foundation and soon a framework began to sprout. Each day there were dozens of workers toiling, steel, heavy machinery and countless stacks of materials dedicated to bringing this picture to life. And of course, every day it became more and more like the picture that still sat in front of it.

Then one day I drove by and the machines and the materials and the workers were gone, but what remained was the picture of the shopping center as it was intended to be - and behind it, the shopping center as it had become. This beautiful shopping center that I had only seen in a picture was there in front of me and it was even more beautiful than the picture. It was huge and everything in detail just like the sign had shared.

As I looked in appreciation of this accomplishment, I thought to myself, "That's the Four Pillars of Success" in action.

Let's break it down:

Intent. The landowner had a specific intent. Not, "I want to make more money." But specific: "I want to build a shopping center on this piece of land." So he hired an architect, an engineer, and together they developed a vision.

Vision. Their vision was so clear, they were able to share it with everyone else on the sign that they created. Then what did they do? They took action.

Action. Blueprints were created of every stage and how everything was going to happen and when. They knew every stage from those blueprints, the dimensions, the materials, and the progress. As the workers followed the blueprints, they did so with complete clarity.

Clarity. If a shipment was late, if it rained or snowed more than it was supposed to, if a machine broke-they continued towards their original purpose, and in doing so, they made the picture that hung over a vacant lot a spectacular reality. They were able to stay focused and maintain their clarity because they were able to look back on the detailed blueprint.

Now that's the Four Pillars of Success in action! Follow this system and you can't fail. This isn't magic; this is a well-based and time-tested foundation of success. Stop just cheering for others who are living their visions. Commit yourself to your own success and follow the steps required to achieve it. Today is a new day. It's your day. Make it a day in which you build on these four pillars.

Don't let your history interfere with your destiny!

Philosophy In Action

How would your life be different if...

You walked away from gossip and verbal defamation?

Let today be the day...

You speak only the good you know of other people
and encourage others to do the same.

Scholars, theologians, and even poets have yet to be able to truly describe and touch upon the beauty, romance, and magic of a relationship built on 100% authenticity.

Beware of the person that is so empowered they ask questions that only actions can answer.

If you can't see what to be grateful for, you can't see what to be great at.

When intent and action mate, the offspring is success.

If you see something different for yourself in the future, you have to do something different for yourself in the present.

Intent and action are the fuel and vehicle in the journey of creation.

Being Free...

The Journey Awaits

The beautiful journey of today can only begin when we learn to let go of yesterday.

Have you ever been on a cruise or looked at one of their brochures? I have been fortunate enough to experience the wonderful journey a cruise can offer. The ships are so magnificently crafted, sculpted for movement, comfort, efficiency, and maximizing the full experience of the trip.

You begin your journey when the ship leaves the dock and moves forward towards its destination. Along the way there is so much happening. There are so many opportunities you can experience and participate in. A romantic stroll along the deck as you look outward to the seemingly endless sea, or maybe you want to go splash around the pool, or maybe enjoy some of the fine food available to you, or maybe you'll join in some of the dancing and partying going on around you, or maybe it's evening and you feel like sitting on the balcony and looking out to the splendid moon and clear starlit sky.

There's so much for you to experience and enjoy from the moment the trip starts that before you know it, you've connected to another dock along the way. Perhaps it's a pristine beach of white sand and breathtakingly beautiful water. Perhaps it's a tropical paradise with tall trees and lush greens that house exotic and precious animals. Perhaps it's a mystical location with a spiritual history and engineering wonder that you couldn't really understand or appreciate until you've seen it with your own eyes.

There is so much that happens when this journey begins. From the moment the ship leaves the dock until the time the ship returns to its home dock, the blessings, opportunities, nourishment, love, laughter, entertainment, and experiences are abundant and immeasurable. By the end of the trip, you are sure to be happily exhausted from enjoying all the journey had to offer. You can go home content that you lived and experienced the journey to the max.

I tell you all of this because it's important to note one thing; one thing that can make or break the trip; one thing that can make or break YOUR journey.

I want you all to understand that NONE of this could happen, not one of those magical experiences could happen if the ship didn't first LET GO of the dock.

How many of you are still holding on to the dock? Holding the dock of yesterday, the divorce, the bankruptcy, the pink slip, the betrayal, the separation, the insecurity, the abuse, the fear, etc...

LET GO! What are you waiting for? The journey, all the magic, all the romance, all the beauty, all the love, all of the blessings, and all of the sights and sounds of this amazing trip through life are here for you NOW. Free yourself from the dock. It's not holding you, you're holding it – let go now! Today is a new day! It's your day. Enjoy the trip!

Live accordingly...
Success isn't
something you have,
it's something you do.

༄༅

Stop allowing your day-to-day life to be clouded by busy nothingness.

༄༅

Your fear of the truth does not hide or dilute it.

༄༅

The more I study, the more I learn and absorb, the more I realize how truly little I know.

༄༅

You are a reflection of nature. You should always be upgrading, refining, and improving.

༄༅

Your life is a print-out of your thoughts.

༄༅

A successful relationship bridges the gap between men and women and that bridge is built with respect.

༄༅

We live in a universe that is always happy to give you whatever your intent-based reality demands.

༄༅

Cultivate Love and Compassion

In this busy world we should never be a stranger to love and compassion. It is the fertile soil in the garden of peace. We must welcome them into our hearts and teach them in our homes. Love and compassion must be cultivated and nurtured like the most precious of our possessions.

Let them embrace all you do. Let them flow like a timeless melody. Embrace love and compassion with all your spirit. Understand that they never hurt or offend, they just heal and empower.

It is only with true love and compassion that we can begin to mend what is broken in our world. It is only those two blessed things that can begin to heal all the broken hearts.

Love and compassion are the mother and father of a smile. We need to create more smiles in our world today. Smiles, after all, pave the way to a happy world.

A smile can touch a person's life in ways you can never imagine. It's infectious and can cause a chain reaction. It can be memorable to someone you pass on the street, or at the mall, or even driving. It only takes a split second to smile and forget, yet to someone that needed it, it can last a lifetime. We should all smile more often.

So give freely to the world these gifts of love and compassion. Do not concern yourself with how much you receive in return, just know in your heart it will be returned.

We need to cultivate true love and compassion.

Remember:
If love is defensive – it's not love.
If love is offensive – it's not love.
Love is pure, kind, and compassionate.

Let's begin today.

It is your belief that you are being held back that holds you back.

Philosophy In Action

How would your life be different if...

You stopped allowing other people to dilute or poison
your day with their words or opinions?

Let today be the day...

You stand strong in the truth of your beauty and
journey through your day without attachment
to the validation of others.

෩

The actions you take today can propel you into a better position tomorrow.

෩

As for your ignorance – do not fear it. Instead be humbled by it and tend to it.

෩

Too much action with too little intent makes for wasteful exertion of energy; and leads to the confusion between movement and progress.

෩

Once your mindset changes, everything on the outside will change along with it.

෩

Don't be disheartened by the forces of evil. Nothing can happen that God hasn't allowed. Even resistance is all part of the grand orchestration. The devil always has you right were God wants you.

෩

Speak the truth! One committed mouth carries the seeds that could change a generation and change the world.

෩

Security Checkpoint

I'm so blessed to have a career in which I get to travel all over the world speaking with amazing people and seeing beautiful places. Along with my travels comes the reality of airport security lines and screenings. Sometimes quick, but often inconvenient, airport screenings have become an accepted and necessary part of our travel process. We all accept the security screening and the inconvenience of it because it is a system that is in place to protect us. It is designed to protect us from terrorists and evils that will harm or hinder our lives.

But now that we have all accepted the need for security checkpoints to protect us from terrorist people meaning us harm, what security system do you have for yourself to guard you from the very real, terrorizing thoughts and fears that hinder you and bring your life to a halt?

Protect yourself! Why let those terrorist thoughts run through your mind free and clear of any security checkpoint? Why let them continue to keep you from living your dream? Why let those terrorizing fears keep you stuck in a bad relationship, or job, or any other condition?

If I have learned anything about fear it's that fear has no substance to it. It's a mental projection of something that has not yet happened. What we call fear is actually pain arising from the expectation that something bad will happen.

What if instead of running from it like you always have, you make the empowered choice to face it? You would strip away the exaggerated expectations and would instead be left with the real components of the situation. Make the terrorizing fear pass through a security checkpoint in your mind. Face it and make it accountable. Ask yourself, "What is true about this situation?" Look at the fear and terrorizing thought on all sides and dissect it so that you can understand its root. This will disarm it and will help you use the fear as an empowering tool instead of a petrifying prison.

Sing the song in your heart
and don't ever let anyone
shut you up!

೫೦೧೩

When forever becomes a place... when forever ceases to be just a word... when it ceases to be just a measurement of time... but instead becomes a place where soul mates can dance to the song in their hearts... that is a reflection of true love.

೫೦೧೩

Some of the greatest lessons you learn in life are the ones communicated without a single word spoken.

೫೦೧೩

If I've learned anything in my life, it's that God has the habit of asking you to do the very thing you think you *can't* do.

೫೦೧೩

When you truly embrace your human impermanence, you connect with the power you have, and influence you have, over the time you have.

೫೦೧೩

Your truth is that you are a creation of God. Your truth can't change; it's permanent. When you can see your permanent truth clearly you'll be able to deal with any temporary condition effectively.

೫೦೧೩

ುುು

You did not go through everything you've gone through just to end up in the same place you were when you started.

ುುು

You can't fully enjoy THESE moments until you let go of past moments.

ುುು

Sometimes the love you'll feel after you've been hurt is stronger than ever.

ುುು

When you stop just existing and you start truly living, each moment of the day comes alive with wonder and synchronicity.

ುುು

Don't just look to keep busy; look to keep fulfilled!

ುುು

Tomorrow is waiting to reveal itself depending on the actions of just one day... TODAY!

ುುು

The greatest antidepressant is gratitude.

ುುು

Philosophy In Action

How would your life be different if...

You didn't allow yourself to be defined by your past?

Let today be the day...

You stop letting your history interfere with your destiny and awaken to the opportunity to release your greatest self.

Poetic Love

My love, though the sunny moments of our days are sometimes darkened by difficult times, our love is the blessed light that guides us to a spiritual bond that can never be broken.

Our hearts dance the sacred dance so many have written of. Embraced by the purest of love, together we stroll along the beach of endless possibilities.

A spirit made complete, I am eternally grateful for the blessing of your love. I pray that I may have the insight to show you how much I truly love you.

A poetic love indeed, it is a tragedy that I have but one life to devote to you.

When your intent and actions are in alignment, you are speaking directly to God.

ℰᏣ

The universe is so well balanced that the mere fact that you have a problem also serves as a sign that there is a solution.

ℰᏣ

Forgiveness is a reflection of loving yourself enough to move on.

ℰᏣ

You may think you are a good person hanging out with the wrong crowd, but to someone watching, the difference is not noticeable.

ℰᏣ

There is nothing like a broken heart to nourish your own sense of self.

ℰᏣ

Nothing inspires honesty like fear or trouble.

ℰᏣ

Do not let another day go by where your dedication to other people's opinions is greater than your dedication to your own emotions!

ℰᏣ

A Time to Take Action

We are at a pivotal point in our great history. The time has come to stop pointing fingers and to start changing lives. Indifference has plagued our society and blame has spread like the deadliest cancer. It's time to care; it's time to take responsibility; it's time to lead; it's time for a change; it's time to be true to our greatest self; it's time to stop blaming others -

Today is a new day!

Today is the day we take charge and LEAD by EXAMPLE!

How could we condemn violence if we're violent? Think about it, at the base of nearly every fear we have, violence is found. It's simply not acceptable! It's never someone else's problem. Stop pointing and start acting! If you don't like to see violence, let no one see it in you.

Why do we allow ourselves to be both victims and perpetrators of hate? Hate should never be a tenant in our hearts. Let us learn from our children who have not yet been taught to hate. Be quick to evict hate from the precious dwelling of your heart. If you don't like to experience hate, find no hate within yourself.

We're born free; free to think, to grow, and to love. Why would we ever allow this God-given gift to be taken from us? How could we ever choose to take it from another? To be controlled is to be a slave. If you don't like to be controlled, never find yourself controlling anyone.

What good has impatience ever brought? It has only served as the mother of mistakes and the father of irritation. We need to learn and embrace patience. Patience is a holy key that will unlock the door to a more fulfilling life. Behind the blessed door of patience are found better parents, powerful teachers, great business men, wise masters, and a more compassionate world. Think of the patience God has had for you and let it resonate to others. If you want a more patient world, let patience be your motto.

Would you like someone to disrespect your mother, father, son or daughter? Of course not, then why would we do it to someone else's? For some reason, we have begun to think ourselves more worthy of respect than others. Sometimes we confuse our social class with something that actually exists, our humanity. We must transcend the illusion that money or power has any bearing on our worthiness as children of God. We are all equal in the eyes of truth and love. It's simple, if you want the respect of others, you must give them respect.

A life of happiness, peace, and love is all within our grasp. I know the questions are plentiful, but the answers are simple – that's how God structured the universe. We each hold the key to a better today. What we must do is cure ourselves from the disease of blame and indifference and leap into the healthy arms of INTENT and ACTION.

BE the change you wish to see - you can do it!

Today is a new day!

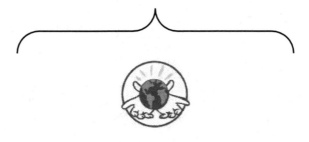

Empowerment is the ability to refine, improve, and enhance your life without co-dependency.

৪৩৫৪

We only have now! Everything else is either imagination or memory.

৪৩৫৪

A lack of clarity is food for failure.

৪৩৫৪

Sometimes silence can be the strongest and most compassionate answer.

৪৩৫৪

Happiness and success come from living in the present, not from existing in the past.

৪৩৫৪

When you live in alignment, you stop telling God how big your problems are and start telling your problems how big God is.

৪৩৫৪

Fear comes from a lack of understanding how powerful you really are.

৪৩৫৪

Decide what you want, create a map, and get your ass out there!

৪৩৫৪

If you want something different, DO something different. Without change progress is impossible.

Your History, Your Destiny

So many of us get caught up in the past: past issues, past relationships, past mistakes, etc... We tend to give away our thoughts and energy of today to days and events that no longer exist. An unfortunate reality of this type of thinking is that we tend to lose sight of our true power and purpose. And we lose sight of the truth that we are free to change – to refine, improve, or enhance ourselves at any moment.

The value of a moment is immeasurable. The power of just ONE moment can propel you to success and happiness or chain you to failure and misery.

What if you could break free from the shackles of self blame, criticism, and disempowered limiting thought?

We all make mistakes, have struggles, and even regret things in our past. But you are not your mistakes, you are not your struggles, and you are here NOW with the power to shape your day and your future.

Today, many will awaken with a fresh sense of inspiration and leave the ghost of yesterday behind, why not you?

Today greets you with no rules or conditions. The only requirement to see all it has to offer is to live it full out. Each day brings immeasurable blessings and opportunities for happiness and success. Like a gift, beautifully wrapped at the foot of your bed each morning, today asks that you open it and enjoy everything inside. Exhaust yourself with all it has to offer! Laugh, cry, say "I love you", say "I'm sorry"; truly LIVE the day... When was the last time you did this? Squeeze all the juices the day has to offer, then, at the end of the day, go to sleep knowing that tomorrow morning another gift will be waiting.

It's when we continue to look into the box of yesterday or last year or ten years ago that we feel depressed, trapped, and defeated. But the good news is that if you just open your eyes and look, you would see today's box, today's gift is waiting. Let go of yesterday, forget it. It's already forgotten you. Embrace the only day in which you have any power; today!

Make a pact with yourself today to not be defined by your past. Instead, shake things up today! Live through today. Don't just exist through it - LIVE through it! Have a plan for success and make sure your actions reflect that plan.

Your dream is a reality that is waiting for you to materialize.

Today is a new day! Don't let your history interfere with your destiny! Learn from your past so that it can empower your present and propel you to greatness.

೫೦೦೪

The greatest sermons are the ones given with a closed mouth and an open heart.

೫೦೦೪

Only when your intent and actions are in alignment can you create the reality you desire.

೫೦೦೪

When you hold a grudge, you want someone else's sorrow to reflect your level of hurt, but the two rarely meet.

೫೦೦೪

This is a mathematical universe. We are surrounded by equations and summations. Your life: the current state of your life, and life itself, is a direct summation of the equation you have created. Your life is a reflection of many choices you have made at the innumerable amount of choice-points you've crossed. Great endeavors are the summation of a great and deliberate equation.

೫೦೦೪

The day you start telling yourself you can, is the day you start knowing you will.

೫೦೦೪

*Don't ever confuse
someone else's inability
to do something with its
inability to be done!*

5 Factors: Take Control of Your Life!

1) Understand that no experience comes labeled, you are the labeler.

The power to choose is yours! As William Shakespeare said, "Nothing is good or bad but thinking makes it so." You and only you are the labeler of your experiences. Do you complain that roses have thorns or do you rejoice that thorns have roses? You have the ability to choose your reactions. All too often the decision to label is not done consciously and your internal dialog will automatically slap on a negative label. You must be aware of this and change it immediately. Realizing your ability to label is an awesome power and a great step towards success. Upon taking control, you can select empowering labels in place of the negative ones. You are in control of the experience.

2) Avoid blaming yourself for making mistakes.

The road to success is always under construction. Every morning we awake to a day we have never seen or experienced. Mistakes will be made and obstacles will appear. You have no control over these events but you do control your reaction to them. It is important that we forgive ourselves for making mistakes. We need to learn from our errors and move on. It is when we hurt that we learn. The power to choose how much we learn is ours. Do you see a stumbling block or a stepping stone? You decide.

3) Understand that like energies attract.

Like attracts like. Positive thoughts produce positive results. If you surround yourself in positive emotions, energies, thoughts, and people, then positive events will be the end result. Unfortunately, the same is true if you surround yourself in negative energies. Do you know someone that is always negative and melancholy? Notice that bad luck seems to continuously follow them. They may say that a rain cloud is right above his or her head. Well, they're right. And as soon as they realize that it is themselves who create that rain cloud they can choose to make it disappear. What you plant, so shall you harvest. If you plant rose seeds you get roses, right? Plant seeds of happiness, hope, success, and love; it will all come back to you in abundance. This is the law of nature.

4) Determine what you want and act on it.

Imagine an archer that did not have a target to shoot his arrow at. He would fire his arrows aimlessly and would not be successful. Have a goal, write it down, and act upon that goal. Now that there is a clear target you can have a plan of action. A visible target is easier to hit. Nobody ever sat his or her way to success. It takes hard work, motivation, a positive attitude and a strong belief that you can do it. That combination produces what we call luck. Do not sit back and wait for life to happen to you. Have a plan and take the needed steps to create what you want.

5) Choose to feel happy.

It has been said, "Act as if and you will become". Try it. It really works. Put your chin up, smile, and think positive thoughts. Remember the happy times and notice all you have to be grateful for and you will feel lighter, happier and more empowered. If you frown, groan, grumble, and focus on everything wrong in the world you will feel down, lethargic and negative. Why bother with that? Identify the things and people that make you feel unhappy and eliminate them from your life. Nothing good can come from them. Choose to be happy and positive. Take steps to ensure a more joyful and positive life. Do happy things, see positive movies, read good books, be around positive people, and practice affirmations. Identify the things and people that bring you happy feelings and surround yourself with them. Cultivate your relationship with yourself and you will be successful. Taking control of your life takes time and requires decisions. The rewards make the efforts worth it.

෧෬

Unfortunately, people often identify themselves by their circumstance instead of connecting with their innate truth.

෧෬

The fear you feel is a direct reflection of the perception you have of yourself.

෧෬

By taking the time to contemplate where you are and where you want to be, you greatly empower yourself. It's a wonderful opportunity to finally set in motion the changes you want in your life.

෧෬

The universe doesn't give you what you ask for with your thoughts - it gives you what you demand with your actions.

෧෬

What I do for a living is talk. What I do for life is action.

෧෬

I am participating in the evolution of inspired action.

෧෬

Time To Renew

Welcome to today! A time to renew, restart, and release.

If you're ready to make a lasting change, you must realize that in order for it to last, it must be a complete change. You can't just renew yourself in your mind and with your words. Your actions must also reflect the new you.

For real, lasting change, you can't just say, "This is a new me. I'm done being the old me. I'm done with people seeing me for the old me. I'm going to be the new me" and then go about your day like you did yesterday.

It won't work.

If you truly want to renew, allow yourself to renew all aspects. It's the only way to create lasting change. Keep this in mind: if the vision you have for yourself in the future is greatly different than your life now, the actions that you take must also be greatly different. You cannot do the same thing and get something different.

Renew all.

Like many of you, I'm on my computer a lot. You know when you're on and the computer has some sort of update it wants to download? Or you open a program and it says it needs to run an update before you proceed? If you notice, when it's done updating, it says, "You must restart your computer" for everything to function properly, to function effectively. When you restart the computer, it has been renewed and is functioning in a manner that reflects the new updates and no longer attached to the old way of doing things.

I understand we are not computers, but there is something we can take from that. When you're sitting at home and you realize that you're done with the old way of doing things and you're aware that you need an update in your life, you must renew - restart.

Don't you ever feel like you need to renew?

Maybe you're done dealing with this person, you're done dealing with that person, you're done being miserable at home, you're done being a smoker, you're done being a drinker, you're sick of living paycheck to paycheck. Whatever it is you're done with, whatever it is you want to update in your life, you also have to restart in order for it to work effectively. It's the beautiful art of renewing yourself.

Please understand that renewing is also releasing.

Are you ready for a new you? With your rebirth there must first be a funeral for your past. Let go! I often speak about letting go because it's so important. Releasing the attachment to yesterday is the best way to renew and embrace the power and blessings of today.

There's no way you can fight today's battles with yesterday's thoughts.

Mohammed Ali once said, "If you think the same at 50 as you did at 30, you just threw away 20 years of your life," and it's so true.

You have to release.

I grew up going to a Catholic church, and they teach you the "Our Father." In this prayer that Jesus teaches it says, "Give us this day our daily bread." THIS DAY, today, "Give us THIS DAY our daily bread." In other words, you can't fight today's battles with yesterday's bread.

Renew, release, let go. Yesterday's gone. There's nothing you can do to bring it back. You can't "should've" done something. You can only DO something.

Renew yourself. Release that attachment.

Today is a new day!

ഇരു

Sometimes I can tell the greatness of my mission with God by the resistance I am met with by the Devil.

ഇരു

One of the most spiritual things that can happen to you is a human breakthrough.

ഇരു

Don't confuse poor decision making with destiny. Own your mistakes. It's ok; we all make them. Learn from them so they can empower you!

ഇരു

When you arise in the morning, think of what a precious privilege it is to be alive - to breathe, to think, to enjoy, to love... then make that day count!

ഇരു

If you respect yourself in stressful situations, it will help you see the positive... It will help you see the message in the mess.

ഇരു

It's not about transcending my humanity, it's about engulfing myself in it.

ഇരു

Philosophy In Action

How would your life be different if...

You approached all relationships with authenticity and honesty?

Let today be the day...

You dedicate yourself to building relationships on the solid foundation of truth and authenticity.

Your greatest self has been waiting your whole life; don't make it wait any longer!

Get Off The Scale!

You are beautiful. Your beauty, just like your capacity for life, happiness, and success, is immeasurable. Day after day, countless people across the globe get on a scale in search of validation of beauty and social acceptance.

Get off the scale! I have yet to see a scale that can tell you how enchanting your eyes are. I have yet to see a scale that can show you how wonderful your hair looks when the sun shines its glorious rays on it. I have yet to see a scale that can thank you for your compassion, sense of humor, and contagious smile. Get off the scale because I have yet to see one that can admire you for your perseverance when challenged in life.

It's true, the scale can only give you a numerical reflection of your relationship with gravity. That's it. It cannot measure beauty, talent, purpose, life force, possibility, strength, or love. Don't give the scale more power than it has earned. Take note of the number, then get off the scale and live your life. You are beautiful!

୫୭ଓ

Never question the power of one! Throughout history it has been the actions of only one person that has inspired the movement of change.

୫୭ଓ

You can still make today the day you change yourself. It's never too late!

୫୭ଓ

It is those of us who have been broken that become experts at mending.

୫୭ଓ

Interrupt your own speaking with your own actions.

୫୭ଓ

Be ambitious towards your own personal enhancement.

୫୭ଓ

Nothing is so unpopular as positive change amongst friends.

୫୭ଓ

Today's a new day. It's your day. You shape it. Don't let it be shaped by someone else's ignorance or fear.

୫୭ଓ

A Life of Freedom

I want nothing more than for all to be free. I want everyone to live a life of unconditional freedom. Think about it, what else could possibly satisfy your soul but to walk free and to BE free?

A life of freedom is one that does not accept "IF," "BUT," "TRY," "MAYBE," etc. It is a life of pure INTENT and inspired ACTION.

The purpose of empowerment is to urge you towards freedom, to help each of you to break free of all limitations. It is that freedom that will give you eternal happiness and finally connect you with the unconditional realization of TRUTH.

I want you to rejoice as a bird in the clear sky, unburdened, independent, and COMPLETE in its freedom.

Imagine a life FREE of fear. Just imagine... freedom from the pains and burdens that can easily manipulate your days. Imagine... freedom from the judgments and stereotypes that blind you from many of life's precious gifts. Imagine... the freedom to just be yourself; to LOVE unconditionally.

My friends; freedom is more than just a word and a patriotic concept. It is the purest intent of God. Love, in its most genuine sense, can only flourish if it is FREE. We, as a people, can only flourish if we are free.

You must free yourself and let YOUR TRUTH have no superior!

With just a simple step in the direction of truth, your spirit will soar.

Do it today! Have no regrets!

Your fear of the truth does not hide or dilute it.

The Strength of a Nation

The strength of a nation is not found in the blind commitment to a political party... It is found in the undying devotion to one's family and country.

The strength of a nation is not found in the celebration of the rich and famous... It is found in the acknowledgment and assistance of its poor and forgotten.

The strength of a nation is not found in the mass symbolic ceremonial praise of God... It is found in each individual's dedication to God's word and law.

The strength of a nation is not found in banks, stores, safes, board rooms, and conventions... It is found in homes, in schools, and in the heart of each individual willing to make a difference.

The strength of a nation is not found in the ability to wage war or keep peace... It is found in the wisdom and purity that sees no need for either.

The strength of a nation is not found on a flag or in its written history... It is found in the love, compassion, kindness, and generosity of each of its citizens.

৪৩

If you want to achieve your greatest self, be your own biggest fan.

৪৩

A victim mentality is a prolonged form of suicide.

৪৩

It's important to know what you don't want, but it's vital to know what you DO want.

৪৩

People who lack the clarity, courage, or determination to follow their own dreams will often find ways to discourage yours. Live your truth and don't EVER stop!

৪৩

We can't undo a single thing we have ever done, but we can make decisions today that propel us to the life we want and towards the healing we need.

৪৩

When you understand the Good Book to be one that isn't necessarily filled with stories to be believed, but instead messages to be received - you free yourself from the burden of previous ignorance and agendas, and you allow the activation of living truth within.

৪৩

Choosing Happiness

What if you placed fewer conditions on your own happiness?

What if you didn't place destination markers on your own happiness? "I'll be happy when I get home" or "I'll be happy when I pay off my house" or "I'll be happy when I have a new car," etc...

What if you change the rules and make happiness a natural way of living?

Remember, nothing in life comes labeled, YOU are the labeler.

You can complain that roses have thorns or you can celebrate that thorns have roses. It's up to you!

Take some time to reflect on the power you possess to control your labels.

This universe is balanced. There is always something you can see as a positive in any situation.

Throughout history, some of the greatest messages have come out of the greatest messes.

Happiness is a gift just waiting to be unwrapped. It needs to be found. And finding happiness should not be seen as finding a needle in a haystack. Each day is a blessing that brings an abundance of happiness.

Finding happiness should be like finding a gift in a stack of gifts.

Find your gift today. It's a new day!

There is nothing more dangerous to the shackles of complacency and the warden of fear than philosophy in action.

৪০৫৪

Are you leaving evidence that you appreciate today or are you only leaving evidence that you are scared of tomorrow?

৪০৫৪

Your seed is your initial intent and it flourishes when your actions reflect that intent.

৪০৫৪

Don't augment your complaints, augment your actions.

৪০৫৪

Fear is a mental projection of something that has not happened.

৪০৫৪

The journey of change doesn't begin when you intend, it begins when you move.

৪০৫৪

A lot of the things you cry about in the present are the things you will laugh about in the future.

৪০৫৪

I am complete, but I'm not finished.

৪০৫৪

ഌര

It's time to stop just talking, it's time to stop just intending, it's time for action; it's time to shut-up and say something!

ഌര

Participate in your own dreams, don't just say what you want or complain about what you don't have.

ഌര

The best way to celebrate your freedom is to LIVE it! Be you. Be free. Don't just make freedom something you have, make it something you do... something you ARE!

ഌര

I don't want you to be the victim of circumstance; I want you to be the owner of the moment.

ഌര

Your capacity to own something is your capacity to change something.

ഌര

Seizing the power of now is what will help you propel your life to where you need to be.

ഌര

Let Today Be That Day

Today, you awaken to a day in which you have the power to make and inspire change.

What will you do with today?

Will you finally break free from the victim mentality and take control of your life?

You have been blessed with immeasurable power to make positive changes in your life. Change things up today!

You will never convince me that we go through everything we go through just to end up where we were when we started. We are here to evolve... to refine and improve ourselves... to inspire and help others do the same.

Today is a new day!

What will you make of today?

The day that complaining about your situation is replaced by actions correcting it... let today be that day!

The day you choose to transcend from the rut of disempowered existing and embrace the beauty of empowered living... let today be that day!

The day you finally release yourself from the prison of past grudges and anger and open your eyes to your current blessings... let today be that day!

The day you stop attracting negativity into your life and enhance your mindset creating a magnet for success, excellence, and positive people... let today be that day!

The day you stop placing unrealistic rules and conditions for your own happiness and realize that happiness is not the absence of problems, it's the ability to deal with them... let today be that day!

The day you stop being haunted be the ghost of yesterday and stop being stressed by the to-do list of tomorrow and just take in all the wonder, beauty, and blessings of our most precious gift, today... let today be that day!

The day you stop having a conflict between your actions and your goals and finally align your greatest intent with your purposeful actions creating a universal symphony serenading your success... let today be that day!

And finally, the day you stop just existing and choose to start truly living... let today be that day!

Today is a new day!

℘℘

The empowered mind allows problems to seed personal growth.

℘℘

Interrupt your thoughts of "I should," with your action of doing.

℘℘

It is your belief that you are being held back that holds you back.

℘℘

It's actually in simplifying life that you get the greatest strength.

℘℘

The universal law of generosity ensures both the giver and recipient profit.

℘℘

When you change for the better, the people around you will be inspired to change also... but only after doing their best to make you stop.

℘℘

The most powerful relationship you will ever have is the relationship with yourself.

℘℘

About Steve Maraboli

Dr. Steve Maraboli is a life-changing Speaker, bestselling Author, and Behavioral Science Academic. His empowering and insightful words have been shared and published throughout the world in more than 25 languages.

Dr. Steve has delivered his inspiring, entertaining, and unforgettable speeches in over 30 countries, earning numerous awards while being enthusiastically praised by media. His quotes and videos have become a social media sensation, being shared by millions across the globe.

Dr. Steve is the Director of the *American Institute for Behavioral Science Education* in New York and is a Board Member of the *Michael Thomas Research Center for Social & Behavioral Science.*

He is a professional contributor to several media outlets, and oversees his philanthropic organization, A Better Today International, which has empowerment, education, and humanitarian programs in over 40 countries.

He is the creator of Psycho-Neuro-Actualization™; a breakthrough counseling/coaching methodology that has gained world-wide attention for its effectiveness in influence and personal/group mindset adjustment. PNA has been called, "The Science of Influence" and "The Science of Excellence," but Steve jokingly refers to it as, "The science of getting out of your own way."

With 15+ years of successful experience as a Business Consultant, Executive/Leadership Coach, and Peak Performance Coach, Dr. Steve Maraboli works with his clients at his private practice in Port Washington, Long Island or world-wide through Skype. (800) 445-0921

One of the most quoted living writers; Steve is the author of several international bestsellers.

www.stevemaraboli.com

www.twitter.com/stevemaraboli

www.facebook.com/authorstevemaraboli

Psycho-Neuro-Actualization ™
"The Science of Influence"

The ONLY Coaching Certification approved by:
American Institute for Behavioral Science Education

Dr. Maraboli now offers training and an accredited certification to professionals looking to separate themselves from the pack.

CALL TODAY - (800) 445-0921 - to become amongst the elite professionals certified in the world's most effective system of influence!

Accredited & Professional Certification Courses for:

- Mental Health Professionals
- Personal, Professional, & Life Coaches
- Sales Professionals
- Speakers, Writers, & Influencers

www.stevemaraboli.com

A Better Today International

A Better Today International is a private philanthropic organization dedicated to creating educational, empowerment, and humanitarian programs across the globe.

Started in 1997 with just a simple website and by handing out flyers at a local train station, A Better Today International has rapidly grown and its programs and charitable works have gained international reach and recognition. Today, A Better Today International has programs running all across the USA as well as in over 45 countries world-wide.

A self-funded empowerment and humanitarian organization, A Better Today International uses its own profits to fund its programs and has volunteers that number in the thousands globally.

Steve Maraboli & A Better Today International have received numerous awards and recognition including from 3 U.S. Presidents and the United Nations.

A Better Today Publishing

A Better Today Publishing is dedicated to publishing books and media that empower, inspire, and educate.

Visit us at: **www.abettertodaypublishing.com**

For more information please contact us at:

A Better Today Publishing
P.O. Box 1433
Port Washington, NY 11050
(800) 597-9103
www.abettertodaypublishing.com

Made in the USA
San Bernardino, CA
15 November 2016